Octopuses

by **Trudi Strain Trueit**

Reading Consultant: Nanci R. Vargus, Ed.D.

Marshall Cavendish
Benchmark
New York

Picture Words

 bottle

 can

 coral

 octopus

 octopuses

rocks

sand

seaweed

shell

 are shy.

An  hides in .

An  hides in .

An  hides in .

An  hides in .

An  hides in a .

An  hides in a .

An  hides in a .

Can you find an ?

Words to Know

coral (KOR-uhl)
a hard substance made up of the
skeletons of many tiny sea animals

hides (HIDES)
keeps out of sight

octopus (AHK-tuh-pus)
a sea animal that has a soft body
and eight long arms

seaweed (SEE-weed)
a plant that grows in the ocean

Find Out More

Books

Herriges, Ann. *Octopuses*. Minneapolis, MN: Bellwether Media, 2007.

Levy, Janey. *Discovering Coral Reefs*. New York: PowerKids Press, 2008.

Markert, Jenny. *Octopuses*. Mankato, MN: The Child's World, 2008.

DVDs

Imax Deep Sea, Warner Home Video, 2006.

Ocean Life, PBS Kids, Lancit Media, 2008.

Websites

Monterey Bay Aquarium
www.mbayaq.org

Save Our Seas for Kids
www.saveourseas.com/minisites/kids/82.html

Smithsonian National Zoological Park
http://nationalzoo.si.edu/Animals/Invertebrates/Facts/cephalopods/

About the Author

Trudi Strain Trueit lives in Everett, WA, near Puget Sound, where some of the world's largest octopuses live. The shy, smart octopus is Trudi's favorite animal and she writes about it every chance she gets. Trudi is the author of more than sixty fiction and nonfiction books for children, including *Sea Turtles* and *Sea Horses* in the Benchmark Rebus Ocean Life series. Visit her website at **www.truditrueit.com**.

About the Reading Consultant

Nanci R. Vargus, Ed.D., wants all children to enjoy reading. She used to teach first grade. Now she works at the University of Indianapolis. Nanci helps young people become teachers. She loves to go to aquariums with her grandson, Oliver. The octopus is one of his favorite ocean animals.

Other Marshall Cavendish Offices:
Marshall Cavendish International (Asia) Private Limited, 1 New Industrial Road, Singapore 536196 • Marshall Cavendish International (Thailand) Co Ltd. 253 Asoke, 12th Flr, Sukhumvit 21 Road, Klongtoey Nua, Wattana, Bangkok 10110, Thailand • Marshall Cavendish (Malaysia) Sdn Bhd, Times Subang, Lot 46, Subang Hi-Tech Industrial Park, Batu Tiga, 40000 Shah Alam, Selangor Darul Ehsan, Malaysia

Marshall Cavendish is a trademark of Times Publishing Limited

All websites were available and accurate when this book was sent to press.

Library of Congress Cataloging-in-Publication Data
Trueit, Trudi Strain.
Octopuses / by Trudi Strain Trueit.
    p. cm. — (Benchmark rebus. Ocean life)
Includes bibliographical references.
Summary: "A simple introduction to octopuses using rebuses"—Provided by publisher.
ISBN 978-0-7614-4892-1
1. Octopuses—Juvenile literature. 2. Rebuses—Juvenile literature. I. Title.
QL430.3.O2T78 2010
594'.56—dc22
2009025935

Editor: Christina Gardeski
Publisher: Michelle Bisson
Art Director: Anahid Hamparian
Series Designer: Virginia Pope

Photo research by Connie Gardner
Cover photo by Stuart Westmorland/*Corbis*

The photographs in this book are used by permission and through the courtesy of: *Art Life Images*: pp. 5, 15 age fotostock; p. 13 Mark Conlin. *Getty Images*: p. 2 Dave King, bottle; Martin Diebel, can; Darryll Leniuk, coral; Don Farrall, octopus; p. 3 Anna Grossman, rocks; Jodie Coston, sand; Micha Pawlitzki, seaweed; Sugar and Sons, shell; p. 7 Altrendo Travel; p. 9 DEA/S Montanari. *Minden Pictures*: p. 11 Chris Newbert; p. 21 Fred Bavendam. *Photo Researchers*: pp. 17, 19 Georgette Douwma.

Printed in Malaysia (T)
1 3 5 6 4 2